BOOK 2

Everyone's a LEADER

Promote pupil leadership in the classroom and give every child the chance to shine!

We're going the right way!

THE PLAY BUS

Age 8–11 | Scott Balliet

Title:	Everyone's a Leader Book 2: Ages 8-11
Author:	Scott Balliet
Editor:	Tanya Tremewan
Designer:	Freshfields Graphic Design
Book code:	PB00112
ISBN:	978-1-908735-91-1
Published:	2012
Publisher:	TTS Group Ltd
	Park Lane Business Park
Kirkby-in-Ashfield
Notts, NG17 9GU
Tel: 0800 318 686
Fax: 0800 137 525
Websites:	www.tts-shopping.com
Copyright:	Text: © Scott Balliet, 2010
Edition and Illustrations: © TTS Group Ltd, 2012

About the author

Since Scott Balliet started his teaching career in the United States of America, he has taught thousands of students from all over the world on three different continents. Currently based in Victoria, Australia, he supervises a student-run school television programme and helps teachers and students with their film-making skills on a daily basis. Since winning the Victorian Curriculum Innovations Award, Scott has also made presentations to hundreds of teachers interested in using multimedia effectively within the classroom and is keen to share his ideas with educators around the world. Having always been interested in personal development, success and effective leadership, he has also combined his vast teaching and film-making experiences to create a whole-school student leadership model, which has culminated in this series.

Copyright notice:

All right reserved. This book is sold subject to the condition that it shall not, by way of trade or otherwise, be lent, hired out or otherwise circulated without the publisher's prior consent in any form of binding or cover other than that in which it is published and with a similar condition, including this condition, being imposed upon the subsequent purchaser.

No part of this publication may be reproduced, stored in a retrieval system, or transmitted, in any form or by any means, electronic, mechanical, photocopying, recording or otherwise, without the prior permission of the publisher. This book remains copyright, although permission is granted to copy pages where indicated for classroom distribution and use only in the school which has purchased the book, or by the teacher who has purchased the book, and in accordance with the CLA licensing agreement. Photocopying permission is given only for purchasers and not for borrowers of books from any lending service.

Due to the nature of the web, the publisher cannot guarantee the content or links of any of the websites referred to. It is the responsibility of the reader to assess the suitability of websites.

Contents

Introduction		4
Lesson 1:	Introduction to leadership and the Student Leadership Code	8
Lesson 2:	Listening	13
Lesson 3:	Empathy	17
Lesson 4:	Attitude	21
Lesson 5:	Determination	25
Lesson 6:	Enthusiasm	29
Lesson 7:	Responsibility	32
Lesson 8:	Sensible choices	36
Lesson 9:	Humour	43
Lesson 10:	Integrity	46
Lesson 11:	Planning ahead	49
My Leadership Journal		52

Introduction

Over my career in education, I have had the great privilege of teaching thousands of children on three separate continents around the world. One universal truth that I have experienced time and time again is that all children *can be* and *want to be* great at something. They just need real opportunities to shine along with a little encouragement to get them started. In other words, *Everyone's a Leader* and we as teachers can make a huge contribution to the development of leaders by nurturing the opportunities for greatness in every child, every day.

If your school is looking for a simple yet powerful way to incorporate character education into the curriculum, this series can provide you with a firm starting point – a framework from which you can build countless life lessons throughout the year. I hope the hundreds, or thousands (or even just one) of the children you teach are in some way better off by you trying out the activities and ideas in this series. You are a champion, and thanks for being the type of teacher who makes this world a better place to live.

How this series can help your students

These days, most students spend more waking hours with their teachers than their own parents and, as a result, emotional needs are often left unfulfilled. It's probably no coincidence that low self-esteem, poor attitudes and disrespect for others are commonplace in our society. How often have you seen potential in a child who refuses to see it in themselves?

By providing multiple opportunities for success, starting at the earliest ages, we can work to reverse this trend. It all starts with the belief that deep inside, all students are amazing and that each has a valuable gift to offer the world. This book is designed to help give all students a chance to experience greatness by being a leader within and especially beyond the classroom. One way that it defines being a leader is as "being responsible and doing the right thing even when no one is looking". If you can impart just this one important value to your students, you will do them a great service which will benefit them throughout their entire lives.

In many schools, character education is in theory a mandated topic to be embedded in the curriculum. In practice, it's usually left on the back burner, with the result that young adults enter high school with little or no internal fortitude to make empowering and healthy choices.

If this is the practice in your school, this book aims to give you some fresh ideas to try. When students become leaders, there is no need to micromanage – they become responsible for themselves. Gradually you can place more and more responsibility onto their shoulders rather than playing "traffic cop" all day. When students are given extra responsibility, they will usually see it as a privilege and will think you are the greatest. They may even thank you for it!

If you already have a strong character education programme in your classroom and school – great! The leadership theme that runs through the activities in this book may be the missing piece that fits everything together.

How this book is organised

The ideas and activities have been organised systematically to teach students of a given year level most of the traits they need to become a great leader. Each month you can introduce a new word relating to leadership such as Listen, Empathy or Attitude. (The first letter from each lesson title helps to form the word LEADERSHIP.)

For each lesson, students are presented with a real-life scenario that they must consider and discuss solutions to as a class. Then they have to put their theoretical leadership knowledge to the test each day in the classroom, in the playground and at home. You can also introduce additional key words (such as Courage, Trust or Teamwork) where appropriate to reinforce the monthly theme and build a wide range of skills.

This book presents the progression over the year in terms of climbing a Leadership Ladder, with each leadership trait represented on a different rung. You may find it useful to make an enlarged copy of the poster that follows so that you can display it in your room for reference as students climb higher and higher over the year. You might also annotate this poster with notes that you, peers, parents or carers have recorded about incidents in which a student used one or more leadership skills.

Relevant photocopiable worksheets and templates are also included with each lesson.

Must this programme be taken as a whole-school approach?

Ideally any programme should be reinforced throughout the school to create a common language and consistent approaches from year to year. If you are planning to pilot a student leadership theme in a single classroom or within a selected year level, you should do so with the intention of introducing the strategies and activities to your whole school at a later date.

The key words used in this approach are consistent with those used in Book 1 of this series, designed for Years 1–3. This consistency means Book 1 will lay solid foundations for future classes working with Book 2. If you adapt any material to suit your context, aim to keep the terminology consistent across the school.

Also, please involve the parents and carers in supporting these themes. The more they support and reinforce the importance of creating responsible citizens, the greater value the students will see in it as well. See page 7 for a template of a letter that you might use or adapt to inform parents and carers of the programme right from the beginning. At the end of each lesson in which you introduce a new leadership trait, you will also find a brief blurb that you might use or adapt for the school newsletter to keep them informed about the programme.

What if some students refuse to follow the Leadership Code and the activities in this book?

If one or more of your students refuse to follow the programme, it is likely that they are having problems in other areas in school (and life). Therefore, assuming that they have been properly assessed and there are no other extenuating reasons, you may need to do a bit more investigation and apply some creativity to guide them towards motivating themselves. Perhaps these students have a limiting belief like "I can't do this" or "This is stupid – you can't make me do this!" Ask them – find out what is stopping them from wanting to get the tools to be a leader and achieve success in their life.

Over time and with a consistent approach (and possibly an individual behaviour contract), most if not all students will actually want to join in – as with any other lesson. As a *temporary* fix, you may need to consider incorporating a positive incentive system that rewards students for participating and doing the right thing, such as providing extra minutes of free time on certain days. Persistence, although it can be highly challenging, tends to pay.

What is most important for all students is to have opportunities to experience success and leadership roles. As well as providing these opportunities while teaching the lessons, you will assist your students by reinforcing the ideas in this book frequently at appropriate teachable moments throughout the year.

Happy teaching!

Climbing the Leadership Ladder

- **P**lanning ahead
- **I**ntegrity
- **H**umour
- **S**ensible
- **R**esponsibility
- **E**nthusiasm
- **D**etermination
- **A**ttitude
- **E**mpathy
- **L**istening

Letter to parents and carers

(Date)

Dear Parents and Carers,

I hope you have been having a great week.

The reason for this letter is to explain a very exciting programme that our school has started, which we would greatly appreciate your support with at home. The programme, "Everyone's a Leader", is a way to build leadership skills in every child, as well as other skills and qualities like confidence, responsibility and teamwork skills. The whole school is taking on this theme, and we would love your help.

Our belief is that every child has a special area in which they can be a leader, and we hope to provide your child with many opportunities to build their leadership skills every day. Each month we will be presenting a new leadership concept to help build up their skills, as shown in the diagram.

All students will have a copy of My Leadership Journal, in which they will keep track of all the themes shown above. We also have developed a Student Leadership Code, and we would greatly appreciate it if you could reinforce it at home. This is our code:

Student Leadership Code

1. I am a leader.
2. I help others.
3. I do the right thing even when no one is looking.
4. I plan ahead and think of solutions.
5. I encourage others to do the right thing.

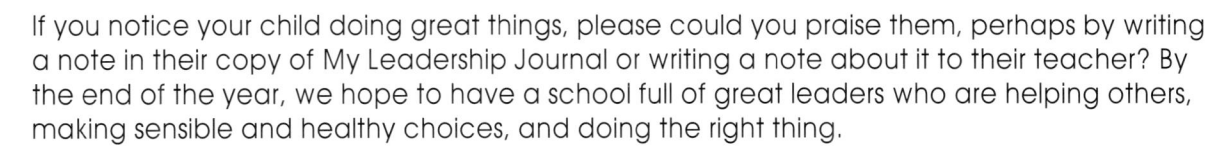

If you notice your child doing great things, please could you praise them, perhaps by writing a note in their copy of My Leadership Journal or writing a note about it to their teacher? By the end of the year, we hope to have a school full of great leaders who are helping others, making sensible and healthy choices, and doing the right thing.

Also, throughout the year, we hope to invite other leaders in the community to speak at our school. So if you or someone you know might be interested in being a speaker, we'd love to hear from you.

If you have any questions, please feel free to contact me at any time.

Sincerely,

LESSON 1:

Introduction to leadership and the Student Leadership Code

Introducing the programme

With the students gathered in a circle, say something like the following:

> Congratulations, students! You've made it to Year (4, 5, 6). This year, we will continue (or start) the leadership training that is going on throughout this school to help every student reach their full potential as a leader.
>
> Now that you are in a higher year, you will have many more opportunities available to you to use good leadership skills. With these opportunities come responsibilities – everyone is expected to make good choices because you are role models for the whole school.
>
> Each month, you will be reviewing and practising a new leadership character trait on our Leadership Ladder. (Show them the Leadership Ladder poster.)

Discussion Introducing leadership

Move on to introduce the first discussion topic:

> Perhaps we should have a quick discussion about what a leader is or how a leader influences others. I'd like you all to be able to lead a discussion, so I've got some cue cards here with some key questions on them to help you. Would anyone like to lead the first discussion on what a leader is? You will need to read the cue card and then call on different students to answer the questions. Remember to always give a positive comment to anyone who volunteers an answer. Before I choose our first leader, I will model with the first question.

Ask the first question on the Discussion 1 cue card (see below) and lead the class in a discussion of their response to it. Then choose a student to continue leading the discussion, referring to the questions on the cue card. When they have finished, congratulate the student, "Great job (student's name), you showed real leadership in leading that discussion."

Discussion 1 cue card

What is a leader?

How does a leader help others?

Why do we need leaders in our home, school and society?

In what ways can students be leaders?

Name some famous leaders (living now or in the past). Why are they famous?

Lesson 1: Introduction to leadership and the Student Leadership Code

Discussion: How we can be leaders

Ask your students to take a minute to think quietly of some ways in which they can be a leader at home, a leader at school, a leader in their community and a leader outside their community. If you choose, they can discuss their responses in pairs as well.

Choose a student (or ask for a volunteer) to lead the next discussion. Explain that the leader will be reading each question and calling on the rest of the class to discuss their answers. You may find it useful to write down students' ideas in a chart yourself to moderate the discussion and to keep the lesson flowing. Alternatively your class may be at a level of ability where you could ask students to write or type the answers for you.

Discussion 2 cue card

How can we be leaders in our home?

How can we be leaders in our school?

How can we be leaders in our community?

How can we be leaders outside our community?

When you have finished, you and your students should have produced a chart along the lines of the sample below.

Sample chart: How can we be leaders?

How can we be leaders in our home?	How can we be leaders in our school?	How can we be leaders in our community?	How can we be leaders outside our community?
Hang up my bag each day	Class duties (office deliveries, line leader etc)	Help with cleaning up litter	Contact schools overseas via email and create a buddy programme
Take care of my pets	Keep my desk organised	Visit older people	Organise a fundraiser to help students overseas
Chores (make my bed, do dishes etc)	Listen to the teacher	Sing in local choir	Contact leaders to change some policies
Help brothers/sisters with homework	Help as a peer mediator	Join a community group	Create films to help others learn

Lesson 1: Introduction to leadership and the Student Leadership Code

Finish off this part of the lesson by thanking the student leading the discussion and then affirming the class as a whole:

> As you can see, there are so many ways in which you can be leaders. Children even younger than yourselves have had a tremendous impact on the world – some have written books, started businesses, starred in films, and created community action groups. So don't ever think you are too young to make a difference. You may or may not know it, but deep inside you have something great to offer the world, and this year you'll have lots of opportunities to do just that.

Introducing the Student Leadership Code

Explain to the class:

> Before we go any further, we need to talk about something very, very important to anyone if they are to become a leader: our school's Student Leadership Code.

The following outline sets out the basic approach you could now take in introducing and exploring this concept. However, if this is the first year in which all or many of your students are learning about the student leadership theme, you may need to expand on it a bit further.

Ask if anyone knows what a code is and explore their current understandings. Explain that *code* has several meanings and write one of them on the board:

> Code = a set of rules

Explain:

> Today you are going to learn an important set of rules called the Student Leadership Code. To be a leader, there are certain things that we must do, so it is useful to have a code to follow. Remember that being a leader doesn't mean that you always are in front of the classroom doing things – you can be a leader in all kinds of ways such as by showing others how to listen properly, or doing the right thing even when no one is looking. To help you throughout the year, we will use the Student Leadership Code quite often.

Show the code and ask the class to read it through with you.

Sample code – unsigned

Our school's Student Leadership Code

1. I am a great leader.
2. I help others.
3. I do the right thing even when no one is looking.
4. I plan ahead and think of solutions.
5. I encourage others to do the right thing.

Tip: Ideally the students will "create" any classroom statements like these themselves to gain a greater sense of ownership. However, any statements they come up with should be consistent with those of other classes if you are adopting a whole-school approach.

Review each statement to check for understanding. Students can then close their eyes and try to repeat each statement, one at a time. Once everyone clearly understands the Student Leadership Code, ask all students to sign it to seal the deal.

Lesson 1: Introduction to leadership and the Student Leadership Code

Sample code – signed

Our school's Student Leadership Code	
1. I am a great leader. 2. I help others. 3. I do the right thing even when no one is looking. 4. I plan ahead and think of solutions. 5. I encourage others to do the right thing.	*Rhett* *Tahlia* Ashwini *Thomas*

Once you have made copies of the signed Student Leadership Code, give it a high profile by:

- displaying it in a prominent position in the classroom so you can easily reinforce students' behaviour when they are being great leaders on a daily basis
- giving the Student Leadership Code to parents and carers too so they can reinforce these concepts at home
- if you are adopting a whole-school approach, posting the code in corridors and other thoroughfares around the school.

Remember to use the Student Leadership Code as much as possible when there is a teachable moment to reinforce its concepts. For example, you might ask:

Are you being a leader right now?

Are you helping others right now?

Are you doing the right thing even when no one is looking?

A strong reinforcer is for older students who have had leadership training to compliment younger students when they notice them following the code.

In the back of this book is an optional template, My Leadership Journal, in which students can record the times when they showed leadership in and outside of school. Parents and peers are encouraged to write comments as well.

Introducing the Emotion-meter

Based on the concept of a thermometer, an Emotion-meter (see the template on the next page) is a simple graphic for students to "show" how they feel on a given day. Students can move a small star up or down the Emotion-meter, giving you and them a quick indication of areas in which they feel confident and those with which they may need some extra assistance. The Emotion-meter may be used to rate feelings, especially in relation to the different leadership traits covered in this programme.

Introduce the Emotion-meter. Explain:

This Emotion-meter is a tool that we use to become more aware of our emotions. If you are feeling overjoyed, you would move the star to the top, like this (demonstrate). If you are feeling so angry that you are being hateful, you would move the star to the bottom, like this (demonstrate). Or you might be feeling somewhere in between, so you would move the star to some place in the middle.

Tip: If it suits the needs of your students better, you might introduce the Emotion-meter in a later lesson.

Lesson 1: Introduction to leadership and the Student Leadership Code

The Emotion-meter: how are you feeling?

Place the star next to the place on the meter that shows how you are feeling.

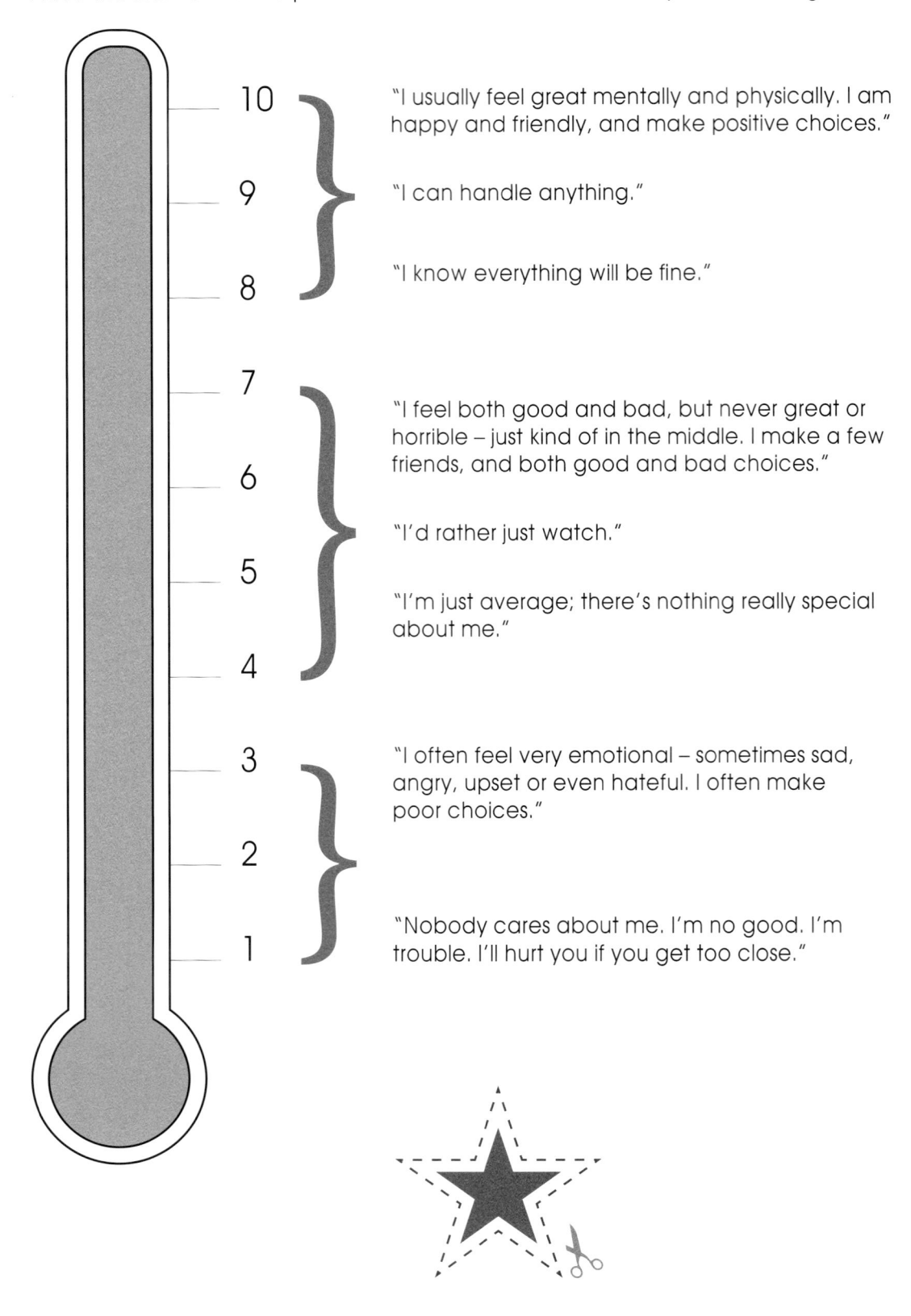

10 — "I usually feel great mentally and physically. I am happy and friendly, and make positive choices."

9 — "I can handle anything."

8 — "I know everything will be fine."

7 —
"I feel both good and bad, but never great or horrible – just kind of in the middle. I make a few friends, and both good and bad choices."

6 — "I'd rather just watch."

5 — "I'm just average; there's nothing really special about me."

4 —

3 — "I often feel very emotional – sometimes sad, angry, upset or even hateful. I often make poor choices."

2 —

1 — "Nobody cares about me. I'm no good. I'm trouble. I'll hurt you if you get too close."

LESSON 2:

Listening

LEADERSHIP

Activity Defining listening

Write an inspirational quote about listening on the board and underline the key word:

> We have two ears and one mouth so that we can <u>listen</u> twice as much as we speak.
> *Epictetus*

Ask your students to write the definition of the underlined word in their own words, using a dictionary or thesaurus if they need to. They then discuss the meaning of the quote in pairs or small groups before giving their interpretation to the class in their own words.

Tip: Students could bring in related quotes and you might share fables or short inspirational stories that involve the concept and tell of leaders who students can relate to.

Activity Reading, drama and problem-solving

Hand out copies of the following scenario and ask students to read it to themselves. Allocate a student to each role and have a brief role play in front of the class. Then divide the class into groups to discuss what the peer mediator should do to demonstrate how the leadership skill of listening could help solve this problem (see the next page for possible ways to prompt discussion). Finally discuss everyone's conclusions as a class.

Everyone wants the ball

Characters (add actors' names)

Sam (Year 2 student) _____ **Jasmine** (Year 2 student) _____

Wade (Year 2 student) _____ **Jen** (peer mediator) _____

Emily (Year 2 student) _____

Scenario: Jen spots four Year 2 students arguing in the playground and others are gathering around them to see what is happening. As she joins them, she hears the following dialogue.

Emily:	Get away! I told you that we don't want to play with you.
Wade:	But we want to play with the ball too!
Sam:	Yeah, you've been hogging the ball for all of lunch time.
Jasmine:	We're allowed to play with this ball – we borrowed it.
Emily:	*(To Jen.)* These boys are trying to take our ball and won't leave us alone.
Jasmine:	Yeah, we checked it out from the classroom and now they say they want it.
Wade:	But the girls have been playing with it for all of lunch time.
Sam:	We just want to play with it for a little bit.

Lesson 2: Listening

Group discussion

What could you say or do to be a leader as a peer mediator, and to help the students in this situation be leaders as well?

Class discussion

What ideas did you come up with to help these students solve their problem?

How could listening help in this situation?

What are some ways this problem could have been prevented?

Discussion prompters

If groups are having difficulty coming up with solutions, you might outline the following steps for them to consider as one possible approach:

1. Disperse the crowd quickly, and politely ask the four Year 2 students involved to follow you to a quieter location.

2. Sit the students down into a circle, smile and explain that they will have a brainstorming session to work out a solution that is acceptable to them.

3. Explain that you, as a peer mediator, are happy to suggest ideas, but you would like them to come up with ideas on their own because they may not like your solution. Outline the two main rules for the circle discussion: first, only one student speaks at a time (the person who is holding the "Talking Stick" can speak or can choose to pass on the Talking Stick without speaking); second, the group is respectful of each person who speaks, which means everyone must look and listen to the person speaking.

4. Once you have heard the facts from everyone, and everyone has had a chance to speak, ask each student to explain how they felt or how they are currently feeling.

5. Ask if anyone has any suggestions that can solve their problem in a way that allows everyone to win. If someone comes up with a suggestion that might work, ask everyone to agree to it. (If any student does not agree, ask them what other approach they think is fair and continue until there is a mutual consensus.)

If groups still cannot think of a feasible solution, suggest other ideas, such as the following:

- The girls who checked out the ball keep the ball for the remainder of the session and the two boys who interfered with their game will be asked to play elsewhere. The students need to agree to separate for the remainder of lunch time until they can all agree to play again nicely.

- All four children try playing a game together.

- The ball will be returned to the classroom and the classroom teacher will be notified that until students can agree to follow some checkout rules, they cannot take any balls out in the playground at lunch time.

- If there are any breaches to the suggested solution, a playground duty teacher will be told.

Tip: Once groups have come up with possible solutions, ask the class to rank the solutions in order from most to least effective. Ask students why it is important to listen to everyone involved in the scenario, and how the children might feel if you did not listen to each side.

Lesson 2: Listening

≋ Activity Reading, drama and problem-solving

Ask students to act out a different version of the scenario to show how the Year 2 students could behave next time to prevent the problem arising. Alternatively, ask students to create their own simple script with their ideas on how to prevent it.

Everyone wants the ball? Let's try that again …

Characters (add actors' names)

Sam (Year 2 student) _____   **Jasmine** (Year 2 student) _____

Wade (Year 2 student) _____   **Emily** (Year 2 student) _____

Scenario: A week later, the same four Year 2 students are arguing in the playground.

Emily: Get away!

Jasmine: We told you that we don't want to play with you.

Wade: But we want to play with the ball, too!

Sam: Wade, maybe she's right. You remember what happened last time. The girls checked out the ball so today it's their turn.

Wade: But I want to play with it.

Sam: Wade, let's do the right thing here. Come on, we can run in the playground – I'll race you!

Wade: You're right. Sorry, girls. Let's go!

Discussion Learning from the scenarios

Choose one student to lead the class through the questions on the Discussion 3 cue card (see below).

Discussion 3 cue card

How did Sam show great leadership in the second scenario?

How did Sam help his friend Wade in that scenario?

How important do you think friends can be in helping to show you the right thing to do?

What might the girls have said to Wade if Sam was not around?

If you were someone in the crowd who saw the argument in the first scenario, when neither Sam nor the girls knew what to do, what might you do to be a leader?

Lesson 2: Listening

Note Listening and classroom management

Explain to the class that to be a good leader you have to know how to listen. This means you have to *stop* what you are doing, *look* at the person talking to you and *listen* very carefully to what they are saying.

Teachers use a variety of Stop, Look and Listen techniques to get their class's attention. Techniques that seem to be effective to quiet a large and noisy crowd (ie, at public events) include raising an arm straight in the air, tapping your head or shoulders, or holding a hand up and counting down with your fingers. These techniques have the advantage of being easy to apply in any situation, in contrast to methods such as ringing a bell or clapping a pattern – if you've left your bell behind or the audience can't hear you clap, you've lost control before you start. Whichever technique you choose, however, aim for one that all staff at school use consistently.

Tip: For activities such as news, or show and tell, ask a student to lead the Stop, Look and Listen technique with the class until the class has fully mastered the art of focusing on the speaker, and showing the speaker full respect.

Daily reminder

Use the word *listen* as much as possible to reinforce the concept whenever there is a teachable moment. If you notice students listening quite well, compliment them on their leadership skills and ask them to record any such occasion in their copy of My Leadership Journal on a daily or weekly basis. If you notice an activity or context in which students need to listen better, ask them, "Do you remember what it looks like to show someone that you are focused and listening? (We Stop, Look and Listen.) Let me see if you can show me that you are listening better now."

Involving parents and carers: newsletter blurb

Leadership word of the month: Listen

As you know, we have a whole-school focus on improving student leadership because we believe every child is a leader. This month, our leadership word is *listen* as great leaders need to learn how to listen to others. Listening means that students Stop, Look and Listen with full attention to what others are saying to them.

If you notice your child listening with undivided attention, please congratulate them and consider jotting this incident down in their copy of My Leadership Journal or writing a note for their teacher to post on the class Leadership Ladder poster.

Thanks and we hope you have a great weekend. ☺

LESSON 3:
Empathy

LEADERSHIP

Activity — Defining empathy

Write an inspirational quote about empathy on the board and underline the key word:

The great gift of human beings is that we have the power of <u>empathy</u>. *Meryl Streep*

Ask your students to write the definition of the underlined word in their own words, using a dictionary or thesaurus if they need to. They then discuss the meaning of the quote in pairs or small groups before giving their interpretation to the class in their own words.

Tip: Students could bring in related quotes and you might share fables or short inspirational stories that involve the concept and tell of leaders who students can relate to.

Activity — Reading, drama and problem-solving

Hand out copies of the following scenario and ask students to read it to themselves. Allocate a student to each role and have a brief role play in front of the class. Then divide the class into groups to discuss how a peer mediator and/or these students could use the leadership skill of empathy to help solve this problem. Finally discuss everyone's conclusions as a class and their ideas on how to prevent the problem (see the next page for possible ways to prompt discussion).

Steph's bad day

Characters (add actors' names)

Jade (Year 5 student) _____ **Tahlia** (Year 5 student) _____

Jessica (Year 5 student) _____ **Cheryl** (Year 5 student) _____

Steph (Year 5 student) _____

Scenario: After a year of increasing arguments, Steph's parents have just told her they are getting a divorce. Steph's dad moved out last night. No one at school knows yet.

Jade: What's the matter, Steph?

Jessica: Yeah, why won't you talk to us?

Tahlia: We're just trying to be nice. Don't be such a grouch!

Steph: I told you, I don't want to talk to you right now.

Cheryl: Whatever.

Jade: She probably broke up with Mikey.

Jessica: Ooh, Mikey! Steph loves Mikey, Steph loves Mikey! *(Tahlia and Jade laugh.)*

Steph: Stop it – leave me alone!

Jessica: Ooooh, Steph's getting angry. What are you going to do, Steph? Huh?

Steph: *(Rushes off in tears.)* I'm telling the peer mediator.

Lesson 3: Empathy

Group discussion

What could you say or do as a peer mediator to be a leader and help the students in this situation be leaders as well?

Class discussion

What ideas did you come up with to help these students solve their problem?

How could having empathy help in this situation?

What are some ways this problem could have been prevented?

Discussion prompters

If the class is having trouble coming up with suggestions for how to prevent the problem, suggest possibilities such as the following:

- The four girls could have listened to and had empathy for Steph, which they might have shown by leaving when she asked them to leave her alone.
- One of the girls could have asked the others to leave on Steph's behalf.
- One of the girls could have asked Steph if she would like to speak in private.
- As the four girls were teasing, they should have done the right thing and stopped.

≈≈ **Activity** ## Reading, drama and problem-solving

Ask students to act out a different version of the scenario to show how the Year 5 students could have behaved to prevent the problem arising. Alternatively, ask students to create their own simple script with their ideas on how to prevent it.

Steph's bad day? Let's try that again …

Characters (add actors' names)

Jade (Year 5 student) _____   **Tahlia** (Year 5 student) _____

Jessica (Year 5 student) _____   **Cheryl** (Year 5 student) _____

Steph (Year 5 student) _____

Scenario: It's the day after Steph has heard about her parents' divorce, and the same four girls are trying to talk with her.

Jade: What's the matter Steph?

Jessica: Yeah, why won't you talk to us?

Steph: I told you, I don't want to talk to you right now.

Cheryl: Girls, I think Steph needs to be alone for a while.

Jessica: OK. You're right.

Tahlia: We're sorry Steph – if you'd like to have a chat later, just let us know.

Jade: Yeah, hope you feel better soon.
(*The girls walk away, except for Cheryl who stays behind.*)

Cheryl: Steph, would you like us to talk privately? Just you and me?

Lesson 3: Empathy

Discussion: Learning from the scenarios

Choose one student to lead the class through the questions on the Discussion 4 cue card (see below).

Discussion 4 cue card

How did Cheryl, Jessica and Tahlia show great leadership in the second scenario?

What did they do to help Steph?

How important are friends in helping to show you the right thing to do?

What could you do to be a leader if you saw the girls teasing Steph in the first scenario, when no one was using good leadership skills?

Extension activity: Community links

With your students, arrange a visit to an aged care facility in your area. Before the visit, have a class discussion in which your students examine their current views of older people and whether they hold any negative beliefs about them. Ask how having empathy might improve the way they relate to older people.

Students prepare interview questions for the residents they will visit, such as the following:

What advice would you give someone in primary school?

Please tell me the greatest lessons you have learnt in your life.

What have been your most exciting experiences or life adventures?

They may also choose to prepare questions for staff who work at the facility with the aim of understanding the happy and sad times of working in this sector. They should also practise their interview techniques with each other before the real interviews.

The wealth of knowledge and wisdom that your students will gather from "refined" citizens will stagger them! Both the older adults and the students will have a memorable learning experience that will inspire everyone involved.

To help make the experience live on for many years to come, small groups of students could record the interviews with a video camera and create a DVD of the visit. Students could then give copies of the DVD to the facility. Some students (with the permission of their parents or carers) may even decide to keep in contact on a regular basis through letters or email.

Tip: If a visit seems too hard to arrange, suggest that each student could interview an elderly person they know, such as a grandparent or a close family friend. Students might even invite older people to school for a day to make them feel extra special. For example, you could hold a Grandparents' Day – with students organising as many of the details as possible!

Daily reminder

Use the word *empathy* as much as possible to reinforce the concept whenever there is a teachable moment. If you notice students behaving with a lot of empathy, compliment them on their leadership skills and ask them to record any such occasion in their copy of My Leadership Journal on a daily or weekly basis. If you notice an activity or context in which students are showing a lack of empathy, ask them, "Do you feel you are being empathetic right now? What can you do to show more empathy?"

Lesson 3: Empathy

Involving parents and carers: newsletter blurb

Leadership word of the month: Empathy

As you know, we have a whole-school focus on improving student leadership because we believe every child is a leader. This month, our leadership word is *empathy* as great leaders need to know how to understand others' feelings. To show empathy with someone, students need to listen carefully to how others are feeling, perhaps by asking questions like: "How are you feeling today?" and "Is there anything I can do to help you?"

If you notice your child acting with empathy at home, please congratulate them and consider jotting this incident down in their copy of My Leadership Journal or writing a note for their teacher to post on the class Leadership Ladder poster.

Thanks and we hope you have a great weekend. ☺

LESSON 4:

Attitude

LEADERSHIP

Write an inspirational quote about attitude on the board and underline the key word:

Our <u>attitude</u> toward life determines life's <u>attitude</u> towards us.   *John N Mitchell*

Ask your students to write the definition of the underlined word in their own words, using a dictionary or thesaurus if they need to. They then discuss the meaning of the quote in pairs or small groups before giving their interpretation to the class in their own words.

Tip: Students could bring in related quotes and you might share fables or short inspirational stories that involve the concept and tell of leaders who students can relate to.

≈≈ Activity   Reading, drama and problem-solving

Hand out copies of the following scenario and ask students to read it to themselves. Allocate a student to each role and have a brief role play in front of the class. Then divide the class into groups to discuss how a peer mediator and/or these students could use a good attitude to be a leader and help solve this problem (see the next page for possible ways to prompt discussion). Finally discuss everyone's conclusions as a class.

"But I'm better than her"

Characters (add actors' names)

Danielle (Year 4 student) _____   **Kathy** (Year 4 student) _____

Brian (Year 4 student) _____   **Andrew** (Year 4 student) _____

Cody (Year 4 student) _____

Scenario: Some Year 4 students are creating a disturbance during a casual cricket game. It sounds like the argument is over who should be bowling. You listen in as the peer mediator. What should you do?

Danielle: It's my turn to bowl!

Cody: Get off! I'm a better bowler than you and we've got to get him out.

Danielle: But it's my turn! You've been bowling the whole game!

   (Brian, Andrew and Kathy, who are also playing the game, gather around.)

Brian: Give her the ball! It's her turn.

Cody: But she's going to lose the game. I'm better than her!

Lesson 4: Attitude

Group discussion

What could you say or do to be a leader as a peer mediator, and to help the students in this situation be leaders as well?

Class discussion

What ideas did you come up with to help these students solve their problem?

How could having a good attitude help in this situation?

What are some ways this problem could have been prevented?

Discussion prompters

If groups are having trouble coming up with some ways to solve the problem, suggest some possible solutions, such as the following:

- Cody needs to improve his attitude towards playing and learn that winning is not the most important thing in this situation. Perhaps the other students could take him aside and explain that to play the game fairly, everyone must have a go.
- The students could all agree to bowl a certain number of overs each.
- The peer mediator could take the cricket ball and bat away and tell the students to work together as a team to come up with an acceptable solution that is fair to everyone.

Activity — **Reading, drama and problem-solving**

Ask students to act out a different version of the scenario to show how the Year 4 students could have behaved to prevent the problem arising. Alternatively, ask students to create their own simple script with their ideas on how to prevent it. (See the next page for one alternative scenario.)

Discussion **Learning from the scenarios**

Choose one student to lead the class through the questions on the Discussion 5 cue card (see below).

Discussion 5 cue card

How did Brian, Andrew, Kara and Kathy show great leadership in the second scenario?

How did they help Cody improve his poor attitude?

How important are friends in helping show you the right thing to do?

What could you do to be a leader if you saw these students arguing in the first scenario, when no one was using good leadership skills?

Lesson 4: Attitude

"But I'm better than her"? Let's try that again ...

Characters (add actors' names)

Danielle (Year 4 student) _____   **Kathy** (Year 4 student) _____

Brian (Year 4 student) _____   **Andrew** (Year 4 student) _____

Cody (Year 4 student) _____   **Kara** (peer mediator) _____

Scenario: The Year 4 students are playing their casual cricket game when the same disagreement arises.

Danielle: It's my turn to bowl.

Cody: Get off! I'm a better bowler than you and we've got to get him out.

Danielle: But it's my turn! You've been bowling the whole game.

(Brian, Andrew, Kara and Kathy, who are also playing the game, gather around.)

Brian: Cody, we need to talk to you. Come here, mate.

Andrew: Mate, I know you want to keep bowling, but what's the right thing to do here?

Kathy: Yeah, is it to win and be a poor sport and make Danielle feel bad? Or is the right thing to be fair to everyone involved?

Kara: We have to play by the rules, and we agreed we would switch bowlers every three overs.

Cody: But I want to win! I'm a better bowler than she is.

Brian: Cody, do the right thing. Otherwise the game stops now.

Kathy: Yeah, and no one wants that to happen.

Cody: All right, I'll let her bowl.

Brian: Cody, that's a good choice, but don't do it with a bad attitude. Do the right thing and mean it.

Cody: Yeah, you're right. (Cody goes up to Danielle.) Here's the ball, Danielle. It's your turn to bowl. Sorry I let my emotions get control of me. No hard feelings, right?

Danielle: Thanks, no hard feelings.

Lesson 4: Attitude

~~~ **Extension activity**   **Community links**

A bad attitude coupled with making the wrong choices can be detrimental to a person's whole life, as many people in the law enforcement field bear witness to on a daily basis. With your students, invite a local police officer to speak to the class about what it is really like on the streets and how most bad situations could be reversed if the people who get into trouble changed their attitude toward life.

Students will also be inspired to see that these modern-day heroes are genuinely friendly people. Your police branch may have an ongoing programme, involving periodic visits to schools to promote trust and familiarity. (The officer who visited our school each month was known by name to all the Year 6 students and the kids could not get enough of him. Imagine the respect he earned through giving an hour of his time each month!)

After the visit, students could create a series of inspirational posters to display around their school. The aims would be to promote awareness of the importance of a good attitude and to encourage others to have a good attitude in all aspects of their daily lives, such as getting to school on time, getting enough sleep, following rules and making great leadership choices.

Daily reminder

Use the word *attitude* as much as possible to reinforce the concept whenever there is a teachable moment. For instance, if you notice students displaying a great attitude, compliment them on their leadership skills and ask them to record any such occasion in their copy of My Leadership Journal on a daily or weekly basis. If you notice an activity or context in which students need to improve their attitude, ask them, "Do you remember the leadership skill called attitude? If we were to rate your attitude on the Emotion-meter right now, can you see that your attitude would appear pretty low down on it and perhaps it could be better? Let's try to make a better choice. Do you need some time to cool down first or are you ready to do the right thing now?"

Involving parents and carers: newsletter blurb

Leadership word of the month: Attitude

As you know, we have a whole-school focus on improving student leadership because we believe every child is a leader. This month, our leadership word is *attitude* as great leaders need to have a positive outlook on the world around them and their own part in it. Students can check whether they have a positive attitude by asking themselves, "What score would I rate on the Emotion-meter?" If you don't know what an Emotion-meter is, just ask your child for a briefing.

If you notice your child demonstrating that they have a great attitude at home, please congratulate them and consider jotting this incident down in their copy of My Leadership Journal or writing a note for their teacher to post on the class Leadership Ladder poster.

Thanks and we hope you have a great weekend. ☺

LESSON 5:
Determination

LEADERSHIP

Activity — Defining determination

Write an inspirational quote about determination on the board and underline the key word:

<u>Determination</u> today leads to success tomorrow. *Unknown*

Ask your students to write the definition of the underlined word in their own words, using a dictionary or thesaurus if they need to. They then discuss the meaning of the quote in pairs or small groups before giving their interpretation to the class in their own words.

Tip: Students could bring in related quotes and you might share fables or short inspirational stories that involve the concept and tell of leaders who students can relate to.

Activity — Reading, drama and problem-solving

Hand out copies of the following scenario and ask students to read it to themselves. Allocate a student to each role and have a brief role play in front of the class. Then divide the class into groups to discuss how a peer mediator and/or these students could use the leadership skill of determination to help solve this problem (see the next page for possible ways to prompt discussion). Finally discuss everyone's conclusions as a class.

"I give up"

Characters (add actors' names)

Robert (Year 5 student) _____   **Rhiannon** (Year 5 student) _____

Martin (Year 5 student) _____   **Jordyn** (Year 5 student) _____

Scenario: Four Year 5 students are in a mathematics group trying to solve a series of tricky word problems. One student, Martin, seems to be giving up.

Martin: I give up. I'm useless at maths. You lot can do it instead.

Robert: Why do you have to be such a quitter all the time?

Martin: What if I meet you after school and we can see who's a quitter!

Rhiannon: Look, forget it. If you don't want to help us, we don't need your help.

Jordyn: Hey everyone, quiet! Mr Thomas is coming.

Lesson 5: Determination

Group discussion

What could you say or do to be a leader as a peer mediator, and to help the students in this situation be leaders as well?

Class discussion

What ideas did you come up with to help these students solve their dilemma?

How could having determination help in this situation?

What are some ways this problem could have been prevented?

Discussion prompters

If groups are having trouble coming up with some ways to solve the problem, suggest some possible solutions, such as the following:

- Students could ask Martin what part of the problem he is stuck on and try to work it through together with problem-solving strategies like using pictures or diagrams.
- Martin could draw on the support from his team to strengthen his determination.
- Everyone in the team could try to have a better attitude when dealing with someone who needs help.

Activity — **Reading, drama and problem-solving**

Ask students to act out a different version of the scenario to show how the Year 5 students could have behaved to prevent the problem arising. Alternatively, ask students to create their own simple script with their ideas on how to prevent it. (See the next page for one alternative scenario.)

Discussion — **Learning from the scenarios**

Choose one student to lead the class through the questions on the Discussion 6 cue card (see below).

Discussion 6 cue card

How did Robert, Jordyn and Rhiannon show great leadership in the second scenario?

How did they help Martin strengthen his determination?

How important are friends in helping to show you the right thing to do?

What could you do to be a leader if you saw the students arguing in the first scenario, when no one was using good leadership skills?

Lesson 5: Determination

"I give up"? Let's try that again ...

Characters (add actors' names)

Robert (Year 5 student) _____ **Rhiannon** (Year 5 student) _____

Martin (Year 5 student) _____ **Jordyn** (Year 5 student) _____

Scenario: The Year 5 mathematics group is working together on word problems when one student seems to give up.

Martin: I give up! I'm useless at maths. You lot can do it instead.

Robert: What's the matter, mate?

Martin: I just don't get this.

Rhiannon: Yeah, it's kind of tricky, but let's work together and do it step by step. That way we'll get the answer.

Jordyn: Which part of the problem are you stuck with?

Martin: Oh, I don't know – all of it.

Rhiannon: Okay, let's have some fun with it – kind of like a challenge.

Robert: Other groups are working on it together as well, so I'm sure there must be a solution.

Jordyn: First, let's look at what the question is asking ... Okay, now we'll draw a little picture to show that.

Robert: Does everyone see that the first part makes sense?

Lesson 5: Determination

≋ Extension activity **History links**

Students may be interested to do some research on the determination of one of the most important inventors of the 19th and 20th centuries – Thomas Edison. Although Edison is credited with 1093 patented inventions, he did not come up with them without hard work and determination.

For instance, Edison and his teams worked for years, sometimes 20 hours a day, trying to make his inventions practical, durable and useful. In an interview a journalist asked him whether he considered himself a failure given his thousands of unsuccessful attempts at creating the electric light bulb. Edison is quoted as replying, "I have not failed 10,000 times. I have successfully found 10,000 ways that will not work."

Tell your students:

> Think of a time when you felt like giving up. Now consider what you could achieve if you had the determination of Thomas Edison!

> All great leaders have determination. It is a quality you need to practise to get strong at – it's not something that you are just born with.

To have a bit of fun with determination, set students the task of "inventing" something of their own. For example, they might design and then make a parachute with the aim of making the parachute that is slowest at falling to the ground; they could test their creations using a coin as the weight. Alternatively they might create a bridge of straws that will support the weight of a bottle of water.

Daily reminder

Use the word *determination* as much as possible to reinforce the concept whenever there is a teachable moment. If you notice students behaving with a lot of positive determination, compliment them on their leadership skills and ask them to record any such occasion in their copy of My Leadership Journal on a daily or weekly basis. If you notice an activity or context in which students need to act with more determination, ask them, "Do you remember what it looks like to have the leadership skill called determination? Let's see if you can show me that you can be determined to achieve something positive."

Involving parents and carers: newsletter blurb

Leadership word of the month: Determination

As you know, we have a whole-school focus on improving student leadership because we believe every child is a leader. This month, our leadership word is *determination* as great leaders need to believe they can complete what they say they'll do, without letting any doubts stop them. Determination is only useful with positive goals, so just remind your children about this quality if they get off track from achieving one of those.

If you notice your child showing great determination at home, in a positive way, please congratulate them and consider jotting this incident down in their copy of My Leadership Journal or writing a note for their teacher to post on the class Leadership Ladder poster.

Thanks and we hope you have a great weekend. ☺

LESSON 6:

Enthusiasm

LEADERSHIP

Activity Defining enthusiasm

Write an inspirational quote about enthusiasm on the board and underline the key word:

> Knowledge is power and <u>enthusiasm</u> pulls the switch. *Steve Droke*

Ask your students to write the definition of the underlined word in their own words, using a dictionary or thesaurus if they need to. They then discuss the meaning of the quote in pairs or small groups before giving their interpretation to the class in their own words.

Tip: Students could bring in related quotes and you might share fables or short inspirational stories that involve the concept and tell of leaders who students can relate to.

Activity Reading, drama and problem-solving

Hand out copies of the following scenario and ask students to read it to themselves. Allocate a student to each role and have a brief role play in front of the class. Then divide the class into groups to discuss how a peer mediator and/or these students could use enthusiasm to be a leader and help solve this problem (see the next page for possible ways to prompt discussion). Finally discuss everyone's conclusions as a class.

Tired of practising

Characters (add actors' names)

Ebony (Year 5 student) _____ **Kevin** (Year 5 student) _____

Bridget (Year 5 student) _____ **Amber** (Year 5 student) _____

Aaron (Year 5 student) _____

Scenario: At practice for the big school play, Aaron looks worried and confused.

Ebony: What's the matter, Aaron?

Aaron: I'm tired of having to remember all these lines for the school play.

Bridget: We're counting on you, Aaron.

Kevin: You've got to do them. Don't give up like you did last time.

Aaron: I didn't give up – I got flu!

Amber: Just learn your lines. The play isn't going to look right if you don't show up.

(The group walks away.)

Aaron: *(Muttering to himself)* I'm sick of this. They can't tell me what to do.

Lesson 6: Enthusiasm

Group discussion

What could you say or do to be a leader as a peer mediator, and to help the students in this situation be leaders as well?

Class discussion

What ideas did you come up with to help these students solve their problem?

How could having enthusiasm help in this situation?

What are some ways this problem could have been prevented?

Discussion prompters

If groups are having trouble coming up with some ways to solve the problem, suggest some possible solutions, such as the following:

- The other students could try to find out why Aaron is feeling the way he is – perhaps he is doubting himself.
- Aaron needs to see that being in the play is a great opportunity. Perhaps the other students could help him to see it this way and fuel his enthusiasm.

≈≈ **Activity** **Reading, drama and problem-solving**

Ask students to act out a different version of the scenario to show how the Year 5 students could have behaved to prevent the problem arising. Alternatively, ask students to create their own simple script with their ideas on how to prevent it.

Tired of practising? Let's try that again …

Characters (add actors' names)

Ebony (Year 5 student) _____   **Kevin** (Year 5 student) _____

Bridget (Year 5 student) _____   **Amber** (Year 5 student) _____

Aaron (Year 5 student) _____

Scenario: At practice for the big school play, Aaron looks worried and confused.

Ebony: What's the matter, Aaron?

Aaron: I'm tired of having to remember all these lines for the school play.

Bridget: You'll do great, Aaron!

Kevin: Yeah, with your sense of humour and a bit of enthusiasm, you'll be an absolute cracker!

Aaron: Yeah. Thanks.

Amber: Say that one line again when you arrive in your pirate costume.

Aaron: *(Hesitantly)* "Ahoy there, me party hearties!"

Bridget: Yeah, that's great! I love that part.

Aaron: *(Louder this time)* "Ahoy there, me party hearties!"

(His friends giggle and pat him on the shoulder as they leave.)

Lesson 6: Enthusiasm

Discussion: Learning from the scenarios

Choose one student to lead the class through the questions on the Discussion 7 cue card (see below).

Discussion 7 cue card

How did Ebony, Bridget, Amber and Kevin show great leadership in the second scenario?

How did they help Aaron have some more enthusiasm?

How important are friends in helping show you the right thing to do?

What could you do to be a leader if you saw the students arguing in the first scenario, when no one was using good leadership skills?

Daily reminder

Use the word *enthusiasm* as much as possible to reinforce the concept whenever there is a teachable moment. If you notice students behaving with a lot of enthusiasm, compliment them on their leadership skills and ask them to record any such occasion in their copy of My Leadership Journal on a daily or weekly basis. If you notice an activity or context in which students need to show more enthusiasm, ask them, "Do you remember what it looks like to have the leadership skill called enthusiasm? I might be wrong but it looks like you are a little down. What can you do so you feel better and behave with more enthusiasm?"

Involving parents and carers: newsletter blurb

Leadership word of the month: Enthusiasm

As you know, we have a whole-school focus on improving student leadership because we believe every child is a leader. This month, our leadership word is *enthusiasm* as great leaders are upbeat and positive rather than grouchy or down in the dumps.

If you notice your child showing enthusiasm at home, please congratulate them and consider jotting this incident down in their copy of My Leadership Journal or writing a note for their teacher to post on the class Leadership Ladder poster.

Thanks and we hope you have a great weekend. ☺

LESSON 7:
Responsibility

LEADERSHIP

Activity — **Defining responsible**

Write an inspirational quote about responsibility on the board and underline the key word:

No snowflake in an avalanche ever feels <u>responsible</u>.   *Voltaire*

Ask your students to write the definition of the underlined word in their own words, using a dictionary or thesaurus if they need to. They then discuss the meaning of the quote in pairs or small groups before giving their interpretation to the class in their own words.

Tip: Students could bring in related quotes and you might share fables or short inspirational stories that involve the concept and tell of leaders who students can relate to.

Activity — **Reading, drama and problem-solving**

Hand out copies of the following scenario and ask students to read it to themselves. Allocate a student to each role and have a brief role play in front of the class. Then divide the class into groups to discuss how these students could use the leadership skill of responsibility to help solve this problem (see the next page for possible ways to prompt discussion). Finally discuss everyone's conclusions as a class.

"It's not my fault"

Characters (add actors' names)

Chris (Year 6 student) _____   **Kyle** (Year 6 student) _____

Bianca (Year 6 student) _____   **Josh** (Year 6 student) _____

Crystal (Year 6 student) _____

Scenario: Five Year 6 students seem to be getting upset just before school.

Chris: What do you mean you didn't bring your project?

Bianca: Yeah, we were counting on you to bring it.

Josh: I forgot, okay? Leave me alone!

Kyle: What are we going to do now?

Chris: Yeah, our presentation is after lunch.

Josh: I don't know. Besides it's not my fault! *(Looking at Crystal)* You said you were going to call and remind me, and you never did.

Crystal: That doesn't matter. You're the one who forgot it!

Lesson 7: Responsibility

Group discussion

What could you say or do to be a leader as a peer mediator, and to help the students in this situation be leaders as well?

Class discussion

What ideas did you come up with to help these students solve their problem?

How could taking responsibility help in this situation?

What are some ways this argument could have been prevented?

Discussion prompters

If groups are having trouble coming up with some ways to solve the problem, suggest some possible solutions, such as the following:

- Josh needs to take responsibility for not bringing the project.
- Crystal needs to take responsibility for not ringing Josh to remind him.
- Josh, along with the other students, could go to their teacher and explain the situation.
- If there is someone at Josh's house during the day, perhaps Josh could call and ask if they could drop the project off at school before lunchtime.
- The students could make their verbal presentation without the project, and show the project tomorrow. If this is not viable, they could ask for an extension and present it tomorrow, accepting any loss in marks they might get for being late.

≈ Activity **Reading, drama and problem-solving**

Ask students to act out a different version of the scenario to show how the Year 6 students could have dealt better with the problem. Alternatively, ask students to create their own simple script with their ideas on how to prevent it. (See the next page for one alternative scenario.)

Discussion **Learning from the scenarios**

Choose one student to lead the class through the questions on the Discussion 8 cue card (see below).

Discussion 8 cue card

How did Chris, Crystal, Josh and Kyle show great leadership in the second scenario?

How did they take responsibility?

What could you do to be a leader if you saw the students arguing in the first scenario, when no one was using good leadership skills?

© TTS Group Ltd, 2012

Lesson 7: Responsibility

"It's not my fault"? Let's try that again ...

Characters (add actors' names)

Chris (Year 6 student) _____   **Kyle** (Year 6 student) _____

Bianca (Year 6 student) _____   **Josh** (Year 6 student) _____

Crystal (Year 6 student) _____

Scenario: The Year 6 students are having their discussion before school, and it begins to get heated.

Bianca: What do you mean you didn't bring your project?

Crystal: Yeah, we were counting on you to bring it.

Chris: I'm really sorry but I forgot. I take full responsibility for it.

Josh: Hey everyone, let's not be so hard on Chris. We all make mistakes. Remember when you forgot to bring in my football last week?

Bianca: Yeah, you're right. Sorry, Chris.

Kyle: Well, let's think together. What are we going to do?

Chris: I'll explain to Mr Thomas that any marks off need to come from my share of the project because I know it was my job to bring it in today.

Crystal: Well, I think I need to share some responsibility too. It was my job to call you this morning to remind you and I forgot as well.

Chris: Maybe I can ask Mr Thomas if I can call home to get my mum to drop it off. If she's not home, maybe Mr Thomas can give us an extension but I'll still ask that he takes the marks off my share.

Activity: Science

If you have a small patch of land near your classroom, your students could create a vegetable patch with some easy-to-grow vegetables like tomatoes, courgettes and beans (or whatever is suited to your climate). Students can organise a roster system in which they allocate various responsibilities, such as weeding the garden and watering the plants each week. Students can also become more responsible for making healthy choices when they eat what they helped to raise.

If a vegetable patch isn't feasible, consider creating a worm farm for the students to tend. Raising worms can teach students a wide variety of lessons – one being that the friendly worm is nothing to be scared of! Students will be reducing the amount of food scraps that go to a landfill, and the worms will convert the scraps into rich dark castings – perfect for any garden.

If you want to go even further up the food chain, students could become responsible for a chicken coop. It will be a popular opportunity to feed and take care of the animals. More than that, the eggs will be rather nice as well – and can inspire an omelette cooking day, complete with vegetables from the garden. (You might want to exclude the worms from the recipe though!)

Tip: As a simpler alternative to the above, students can grow their own plants in the classroom. Nasturtiums, for example, are easy and fast to grow, with edible flowers. Grow the seeds in a clear plastic cup so students can see the root system and check how much water is sitting in the cup. Place at least three seeds in each cup to get at least one surviving plant. (It's also a good idea to plant some seeds in a few extra cups just in case any new students arrive or replacements are needed for any existing students.)

Daily reminder

Use the word *responsibility* as much as possible to reinforce the concept whenever there is a teachable moment. If you notice students showing responsibility, compliment them on their leadership skills and ask them to record any such occasion in their copy of My Leadership Journal on a daily or weekly basis. If you notice an activity or context in which students need to show more responsibility, ask them, "Do you remember the leadership skill called responsibility? What can you do to show that you are a leader who can take responsibility for this?"

Involving parents and carers: newsletter blurb

Leadership word of the month: Responsibility

As you know, we have a whole-school focus on improving student leadership because we believe every child is a leader. This month, our leadership word is *responsibility* as great leaders need to be responsible for what they say and do. For your child, being responsible might mean being responsible for packing their school bag without any reminders, feeding a pet or doing their homework on time.

If you notice your child being responsible at home, please congratulate them and consider jotting this incident down in their copy of My Leadership Journal or writing a note for their teacher to post on the class Leadership Ladder poster.

Thanks and we hope you have a great weekend. ☺

LESSON 8:

Sensible choices

LEADERSHIP

Activity **Defining sensible choices**

Write an inspirational quote about being sensible on the board and underline the key word:

> To have begun is half the job: be bold and be <u>sensible</u>.   *Horace*

Ask your students to write the definition of the underlined word in their own words, using a dictionary or thesaurus if they need to. They then discuss the meaning of the quote in pairs or small groups before giving their interpretation to the class in their own words.

Tip: Students could bring in related quotes and you might share fables or short inspirational stories that involve the concept and tell of leaders who students can relate to.

Activity **Reading, drama and problem-solving**

Hand out copies of the following scenario and ask students to read it to themselves. Allocate a student to each role and have a brief role play in front of the class. Then divide the class into groups to discuss how the peer mediator and/or the other students could use the leadership skill of making sensible choices to help solve this problem (see the next page for possible ways to prompt discussion). Finally discuss everyone's conclusions as a class.

Pushing and shoving

Characters (add actors' names)

Tessa (Year 2 student) _____   **Michael** (Year 2 student) _____

Sally (Year 2 student) _____   **Kara** (Year 6 peer mediator) _____

Joel (Year 2 student) _____

Scenario: Two Year 2 students are pushing and shoving each other in the queue for hot dogs at a school fundraiser. Kara senses that she has to act quickly before the argument escalates.

Tessa:	Get to the back of the line – *now*!
Sally:	Well, give me my money!
	(Both students see Kara and try to plead their cases.)
Tessa:	Sally pushed in front of me in line.
Sally:	Well, Tessa stole my money.
Tessa:	I picked it up from the ground.
Sally:	It's mine!
Joel:	It's true – it's Sally's. I saw it drop out of her pocket when she pushed into line.
Michael:	Yeah, but she shouldn't have pushed into line.

Lesson 8: Sensible choices

Group discussion

What could you say or do to be a leader as a peer mediator, and to help the students in this situation be leaders as well?

Class discussion

What ideas did you come up with to help these students solve their problem?

How could making sensible choices help in this situation?

What are some ways this problem could have been prevented?

Discussion prompters

If groups are having difficulty coming up with solutions, you might outline the following steps for them to consider as one possible approach:

1. Calm the four students down by moving them to a quieter location.

2. Sit the students down in a circle, smile and explain that they will be having a brainstorming session to work out a solution that is acceptable to them.

3. Explain that you, as a peer mediator, are happy to suggest ideas, but you would like them to come up with ideas on their own because they may not like your solution. Outline the two main rules for the circle discussion: first, only one student speaks at a time (the person who is holding the "Talking Stick" can speak or can choose to pass on the Talking Stick without speaking); second, the group is respectful of each person who speaks, which means everyone must look and listen to the person speaking.

4. Most students will want to tell you what happened in their own words in the hope that you will then see why they are right. Once you have heard the facts from everyone, and everyone has had a chance to speak, ask each student to explain how they felt or how they are currently feeling.

5. Ask if anyone has any suggestions that can solve their problem in a way that allows everyone to win. If someone comes up with a suggestion that might work, ask everyone to agree to it. (If any student does not agree, ask them what other approach they think is fair and continue until there is a consensus.)

If groups still cannot think of a feasible solution, suggest other ideas, such as the following:

- Ask Sally, who pushed into the queue, how she thinks her behaviour made everyone behind her feel. Ask if her choice of this behaviour was sensible.

- Ask Tessa, who picked up the money, if she had asked who the owner was. Ask how she might feel if someone picked up her money. Ask if her choice of this behaviour was sensible.

- Ask Joel and Michael, who were observing the argument, if they could have done anything to help the situation, such as asking Sally politely to move to the back.

- Ask all four students if they can think of some solutions now so that they can get back to eating hot dogs rather than sitting in a circle.

≋ Activity **Reading, drama and problem-solving**

Ask students to act out a different version of the scenario to show how the Year 2 students could have behaved to prevent the problem arising. Alternatively, ask students to create their own simple script with their ideas on how to prevent it.

Lesson 8: Sensible choices

Pushing and shoving? Let's try that again ...

Characters (add actors' names)

Tessa (Year 2 student) _____ **Michael** (Year 2 student) _____

Sally (Year 2 student) _____ **Joel** (Year 2 student) _____

Scenario: The two Year 2 students are pushing and shoving each other in the queue, and it sounds like a nasty argument could be brewing.

Tessa: Get to the back of the line – *now*!

Sally: Well, give me my money!

Joel: Hey you two, let's be leaders and make some sensible choices. I saw the money drop out of Sally's pocket so I think you should give it back to her, Tessa.

Michael: Yeah, and Sally you shouldn't have pushed into line so I think you need to do the right thing. Maybe you should make a more sensible choice and go to the back of the queue.

Joel: I think the other thing that should happen is that you both should apologise to each other and shake hands.

(The girls frown at each other at first, then giggle and shake hands.)

Discussion Learning from the scenarios

Choose one student to lead the class through the questions on the Discussion 9 cue card (see below).

Discussion 9 cue card

How did each student show great leadership in the second scenario?

What are some things they did to make a sensible choice?

What could you do to be a leader if you saw the students arguing in the first scenario, when no one was using good leadership skills?

Activity Reading and listening

Explain to the class:

> Today you will learn a lesson that will help you for your entire life. If you follow this simple lesson, you will almost always be successful.
>
> Today's lesson is about making sensible choices. What is a *choice*?

Ask two students to role-model making a sensible choice of a healthy snack when their choice is between an apple and an orange. Establish with the class that in this case either choice is sensible.

Next ask two more students to role-model making the same sensible choice but now they must choose between fruit and sweets. Explain that even though they may have wanted the sweets, the sensible, healthy choice was the fruit.

Lesson 8: Sensible choices

As you hand out copies of "The sensible choices story" (see the master copy on page 40), explain:

> Today is a lucky day as we are going to read a comic strip together on sensible choices. This story will help you the next time you have a tough decision to make.

As you read through the story together, make long, dramatic pauses to help the message from each frame to sink in.

Explain that the next time any of your students is faced with a tough choice, they need to stop and choose the right thing to do. Emphasise this point with the "What should I do?" poster which follows "The sensible choices story".

Daily reminder

Refer to *sensible choices* as much as possible to reinforce the concept whenever there is a teachable moment. If you notice students making sensible choices, compliment them on their leadership skills and ask them to record any such occasion in their copy of My Leadership Journal on a daily or weekly basis. If you notice an activity or context in which students need to make better choices, ask them, "Do you remember the leadership lesson on sensible choices? Do you feel that your choice is going to create a good outcome or an outcome where someone is going to be unhappy? Perhaps you should think about what you did and the effect it had. Now what is a more sensible choice and how can you do the right thing?"

Involving parents and carers: newsletter blurb

Leadership words of the month: Sensible choices

As you know, we have a whole-school focus on improving student leadership because we believe every child is a leader. This month, our leadership theme is *sensible choices* as great leaders need to make healthy choices that are good for them and others rather than make choices that might harm themselves or others in some way.

If you notice your child making sensible choices at home, please congratulate them and consider jotting this incident down in their copy of My Leadership Journal or writing a note for their teacher to post on the class Leadership Ladder poster.

Thanks and we hope you have a great weekend. ☺

Lesson 8: Sensible choices

The sensible choices story

Every day you have a choice.

You always have a choice.

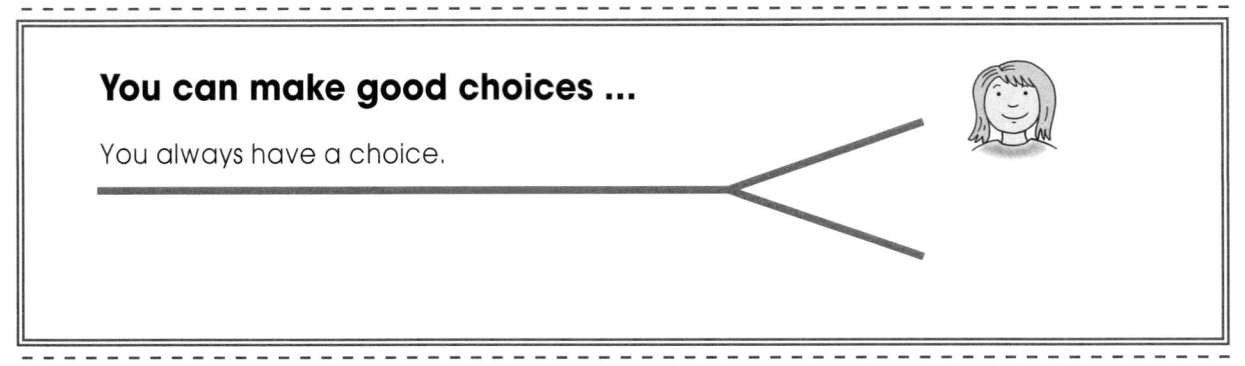

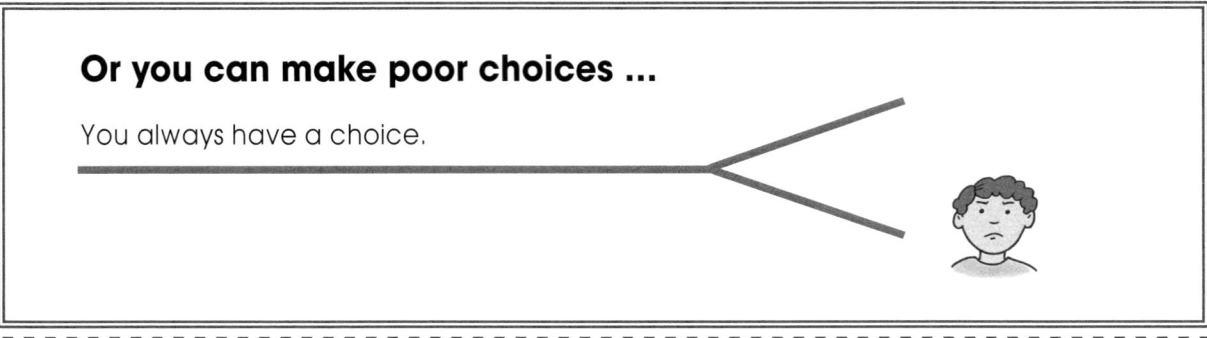

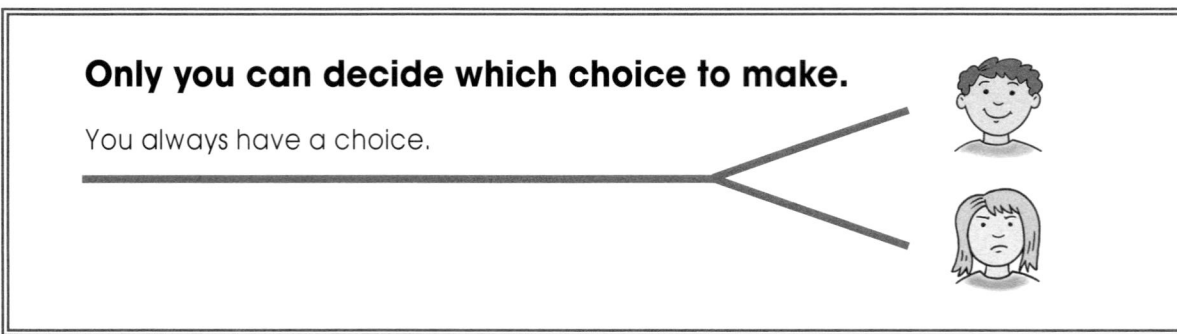

You can make good choices ...

You always have a choice.

Or you can make poor choices ...

You always have a choice.

Only you can decide which choice to make.

You always have a choice.

Some people make great choices for their whole life.

You always have a choice.

These people do the right thing even when no one is looking. They live a happy life.

You always have a choice.

Some people make poor choices for their whole life.

You always have a choice.

They are often unhappy and may not know why.

You always have a choice.

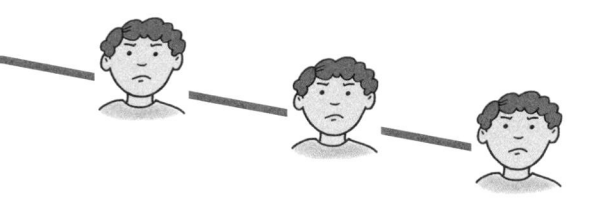

You always have a choice.

Even if you have made poor choices before, you can still change to make great choices ...

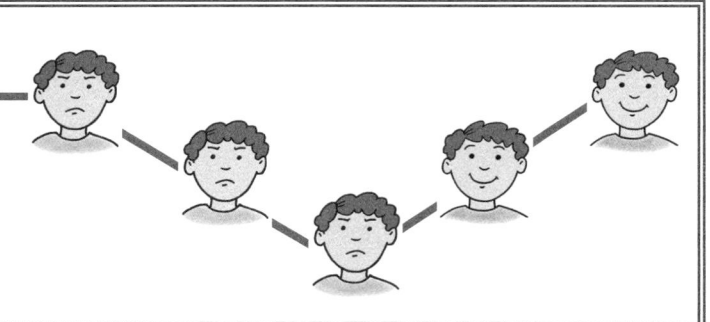

But it's all up to you.

What should I do?

You always have a choice.

LESSON 9:

Humour

LEADERSHIP

Write an inspirational quote about having a sense of humour on the board and underline the key word:

> Every survival kit should include a sense of <u>humour</u>.   *Unknown*

Ask your students to write the definition of the underlined word in their own words, using a dictionary or thesaurus if they need to. They then discuss the meaning of the quote in pairs or small groups before giving their interpretation to the class in their own words.

Tip: Students could bring in related quotes and you might share fables or short inspirational stories that involve the concept and tell of leaders who students can relate to.

Activity — Reading, drama and problem-solving

Hand out copies of the following scenario and ask students to read it to themselves. Allocate a student to each role and have a brief role play in front of the class. Then divide the class into groups to discuss how the peer mediator and/or the other students could use humour to be a leader and help solve this problem (see the next page for possible ways to prompt discussion). Finally discuss everyone's conclusions as a class.

Drenched and distressed

Characters (add actors' names)

Julie (Year 2 student) _____   **Ben** (Year 2 student) _____

Setti (Year 2 student) _____   **Cindy** (peer mediator) _____

William (Year 2 student) _____

Scenario: Three Year 2 students are laughing at Julie, another student in their year. Cindy saw Julie's juice box squirt all over her when she tried to open it. Cindy had to hold back a laugh herself as it did look comical. But she senses that things might soon escalate if she doesn't act quickly.

Julie: Oh no, my juice, it's all over me!

Setti: Ha ha!

William: Look at you, you're drenched. *(Laughs)*

Julie: Stop laughing at me!

Ben: Ha ha!

Julie: Stop it – leave me alone! I'm telling the peer mediator. *(Running up to Cindy)* My juice box exploded and now they're all laughing at me.

Cindy: Okay, let's see what we can do.

Lesson 9: Humour

Group discussion

What could you say or do to be a leader as a peer mediator, and help the students in this situation be leaders as well?

Class discussion

What ideas did you come up with to help these students solve their problem?

How could having a sense of humour help in this situation?

What are some ways this problem could have been prevented?

Discussion starters

If groups are having trouble coming up with some ways to solve the problem, suggest some possible solutions, such as the following:

- Ask Julie gently, "Even though you don't like them laughing, can you see why they thought it was just a little bit funny?"
- Ask Julie, "Have you ever seen any TV shows where people laugh at each other for doing silly things?"
- Suggest to the other students that if they sense someone is getting upset, they should do the right thing rather than making the person more upset by teasing.

Activity **Reading, drama and problem-solving**

Ask students to act out a different version of the scenario to show how the Year 2 students could have behaved to prevent the problem arising. Alternatively, ask students to create their own simple script with their ideas on how to prevent it.

Drenched and distressed? Let's try that again ...

Characters (add actors' names)

Julie (Year 2 student) _____ **William** (Year 2 student) _____

Setti (Year 2 student) _____ **Ben** (Year 2 student) _____

Scenario: Julie has tried to open her juice box but it has squirted all over her. Three other Year 2 students seem to be laughing at her.

Julie:	Oh no, my juice, it's all over me!
Setti:	Ha ha!
William:	Look at you, you're drenched. *(Laughs.)*
Julie:	Yeah, yeah. Great! Now I've got to get myself cleaned up ...
Ben:	Ha ha!
William:	Ben, the fun is over.
Setti:	Come on, Julie, I'll help you get cleaned up.
Ben:	Ha ha!
Julie:	*(Flicks a tiny bit of juice on Ben, laughs and runs away.)*
Ben:	Hey you! *(Laughs and chases the girls.)*

Lesson 9: Humour

Discussion — Learning from the scenarios

Choose one student to lead the class through the questions on the Discussion 10 cue card (see below).

Discussion 10 cue card

How did everyone except Ben show great leadership in the second scenario?

What are some things these students did to act with a sense of humour?

What could you do to be a leader if you saw the students teasing in the first scenario, when no one was using good leadership skills?

If Julie's prank backfires later, how could she make it right?

Activity — ICT

Celebrate comedy by having your students organise a class comedy festival. After researching and writing up some of the funniest jokes and skits (family-friendly of course), they record them using a video camera. They also go around the school during lunch time to record jokes from other students throughout the school. Finally your students edit the film to create a DVD which they can use to share their humour more widely.

Note: Parents and carers will need to sign a publicity release form before children can be filmed. Most schools have these systems in place already, but doublecheck to prevent any videos going on the internet without the permission of parents and carers.

Daily reminder

Refer to *humour* as much as possible to reinforce the concept whenever there is a teachable moment. If you notice students acting with a great sense of humour, compliment them on their leadership skills and ask them to record any such occasion in their copy of My Leadership Journal on a weekly or daily basis. You may need to remind them of this lesson if they are taking things a bit too seriously ("Do you remember that there are some times we shouldn't take things so seriously, especially if we start to become angry? How could we look at this situation in another way and see some humour in it?") or if they are becoming too silly ("Do you remember that having a sense of humour is not the same as being silly and making poor choices? This is the time to make a sensible choice and to do the right thing. Are you ready to do that now or do you need some time to cool down first?").

Involving parents and carers: newsletter blurb

Leadership word of the month: Humour

This month, our leadership word is *humour* as great leaders need to be able to laugh at things, even when events do not go according to plan.

If you notice your child acting with a great sense of humour at home, please congratulate them and consider jotting this incident down in their copy of My Leadership Journal or writing a note for their teacher to post on the class Leadership Ladder poster.

Thanks and we hope you have a great weekend. ☺

LESSON 10:

Integrity

LEADERSHIP

Write an inspirational quote about integrity on the board and underline the key word:

Integrity is doing the right thing, even if nobody is watching. *Unknown*

Ask your students to write the definition of the underlined word in their own words, using a dictionary or thesaurus if they need to. They then discuss the meaning of the quote in pairs or small groups before giving their interpretation to the class in their own words.

Tip: Students could bring in related quotes and you might share fables or short inspirational stories that involve the concept and tell of leaders who students can relate to.

Activity — Reading, drama and problem-solving

Hand out copies of the following scenario and ask students to read it to themselves. Allocate a student to each role and have a brief role play in front of the class. Then divide the class into groups to discuss how the peer mediator and/or the other students could show integrity and use it to be a leader and help solve this problem (see the next page for possible ways to prompt discussion). Finally discuss everyone's conclusions as a class.

"But you promised"

Characters (add actors' names)

Fiona (Year 5 student) _____   **Lachi** (Year 5 student) _____

Zoe (Year 5 student) _____   **David** (Year 5 student) _____

Kaitlyn (Year 5 student) _____   **Jessie** (peer mediator) _____

Scenario: Five Year 5 students are starting to yell at each other. Jessie is just passing by and listens in to find out what the argument is about.

Fiona: But you promised I could use your camera – let me have it!

Zoe: I changed my mind.

Fiona: I only want to borrow it for a minute, just hand it over.

Lachi: Why won't you let her have it?

David: Yeah, you said you would.

Kaitlyn: Look, you three, leave Zoe alone. *(Holds and plays with Zoe's camera.)* She changed her mind so buzz off.

Lachi: You're just saying that because you said you'd be her friend if she lent it to you!

Lesson 10: Integrity

Group discussion
What could you say or do to be a leader as a peer mediator, and to help the students in this situation be leaders as well?

Class discussion
What ideas did you come up with to help these students solve their problem?

How could having more integrity help in this situation?

What are some ways this problem could have been prevented?

Discussion prompters

If groups are having trouble coming up with some ways to solve the problem, point out some of the key elements of the scenario, such as the following:

- Zoe should learn to keep her word and follow through with what she says. However, she also has the right to change her mind, so the others should respect her wishes.
- Fiona, Lachi and David should not make matters worse by ganging up on her in an effort to manipulate her into lending her camera.
- Kaitlyn should not inflame the situation by telling them to "buzz off". It's good that she is sticking up for Zoe, but she should do so in a respectful way.

Activity — **Reading, drama and problem-solving**

Ask students to act out a different version of the scenario to show how the Year 5 students could have behaved to prevent the problem arising. Alternatively, ask students create their own simple script with their ideas on how to prevent it.

"But you promised"? Let's try that again ...

Characters (add actors' names)

Fiona (Year 5 student) _____ **Lachi** (Year 5 student) _____

Zoe (Year 5 student) _____ **David** (Year 5 student) _____

Kaitlyn (Year 5 student) _____

Scenario: Five Year 5 students are starting to yell at each other.

Fiona: But you promised I could use your camera – let me have it!

Zoe: You're right, I did promise, so I'll keep my word. I do think you need to ask a bit more nicely though, okay?

Fiona: I'm sorry – may I please use your camera, Zoe? Pretty please? *(Gives a cute smile.)*

Zoe: Of course you may. Here it is.

Lachi: Can you take a photo of me?

David: Yeah, me too?

Kaitlyn: Zoe, may I please see your camera once Fiona has finished with it?

Zoe: Yes, no problem.

Discussion — **Learning from the scenarios**

Choose one student to lead the class through the questions on the Discussion 11 cue card (see next page).

Lesson 10: Integrity

Discussion 11 cue card

How did Zoe, Fiona and Kaitlyn show great leadership in the second scenario?

How did Zoe have integrity?

What could you do to be a leader if you saw the students arguing in the first scenario, when no one was using good leadership skills?

Extension activity **Design**

Set students the task of creating a class "integrity quilt". Each student will design and create a quilt patch (either out of cloth or paper). Their design is to symbolise something special about them, such as a hobby they enjoy or a goal they might have. Once joined together, the quilt as a whole can be symbolic of how each student is an integral part of the class – all must work together and do the right thing.

As new students join the class over the year, they can create a patch for the quilt so that they feel welcomed to and part of the class. When students leave the school, they are forever linked in the quilt, so that great memories and their commitment to each other remain.

At the end of the school year, take a photo of the students in front of the quilt as a record for each of them to take away. Towards the end of each school year students might also create a special video message for incoming students to help inspire them to always do the right thing. You can also keep the quilt made each year to show the incoming class how it helps to keep all your classes forever connected.

Daily reminder

Use the word *integrity* as much as possible to reinforce the concept whenever there is a teachable moment. If you notice students showing a lot of integrity, compliment them on their leadership skills and ask them to record any such occasion in their copy of My Leadership Journal on a daily or weekly basis. If you notice an activity or context in which students need to behave with more integrity, ask them, "Do you remember the leadership skill called integrity? I know you are a great leader and have a lot of integrity. Deep down, I also know you want to do the right thing. How about you think what you can do to make a better choice so that you make this right?"

Involving parents and carers: newsletter blurb

Leadership word of the month: Integrity

This month, our leadership word is *integrity* as great leaders need be honest and do the right thing, even when no one is looking. When students have integrity, they do what they say they are going to do and people trust them. Integrity is one of the most important characteristics of leadership.

If you notice your child acting with integrity at home, please congratulate them and consider jotting this incident down in their copy of My Leadership Journal or writing a note for their teacher to post on the class Leadership Ladder poster.

Thanks and we hope you have a great weekend. ☺

LESSON 11:
Planning ahead

LEADERSHIP

Activity — **Defining planning**

Write an inspirational quote about planning on the board and underline the key word:

> Good fortune is what happens when opportunity meets with planning. *Thomas Edison*

Ask your students to write the definition of the underlined word in their own words, using a dictionary or thesaurus if they need to. They then discuss the meaning of the quote in pairs or small groups before giving their interpretation to the class in their own words.

Tip: Students could bring in related quotes and you might share fables or short inspirational stories that involve the concept and tell of leaders who students can relate to.

Activity — **Reading, drama and problem-solving**

Hand out copies of the following scenario and ask students to read it to themselves. Allocate a student to each role and have a brief role play in front of the class. Then divide the class into groups to discuss how the students in this scenario could use the leadership skill of planning ahead to help solve this problem (see the next page for possible ways to prompt discussion). Finally discuss everyone's conclusions as a class.

Forgotten farewell

Characters (add actors' names)

Olivia (Year 6 student) _____   **Tom** (Year 6 student) _____

James (Year 6 student) _____   **Grant** (Year 6 student) _____

Christine (Year 6 student) _____

Scenario: Four Year 6 students are talking at lunch time about how they forgot to organise anything for their good friend Olivia, who is leaving today for another school.

James: This is her last day!

Grant: We should have done something sooner.

Tom: I think she knows we haven't planned anything.

Christine: I feel really bad – she's been such a great friend.

James: Here she comes.

Group discussion

What could you say or do to be a leader if you were listening in on this conversation, and to help the students in this situation be leaders as well?

Class discussion

What ideas did you come up with to help these students solve their problem?

How could planning ahead have helped in this situation?

What are some ways this problem could have been prevented?

Lesson 11: Planning ahead

Discussion prompters

If groups are having trouble coming up with some ways to solve the problem, suggest some possible solutions, such as the following:

- The four students could tell the truth and say that they meant to do something but they hadn't planned very well.
- They could spend the rest of lunch with Olivia and tell her all the great things they remember she did for them.
- They should have planned things before but, as they didn't, they could admit their oversight to their teacher and ask for some material to create a card for her during the next break.

Activity — **Reading, drama and problem-solving**

Ask students to act out a different version of the scenario to show how the Year 6 students could have behaved to prevent the problem arising. Alternatively, ask students to create their own simple script with their ideas on how to prevent it.

Forgotten farewell? Let's try that again ...

Characters (add actors' names)

Olivia (Year 6 student) _____ **Tom** (Year 6 student) _____

James (Year 6 student) _____ **Grant** (Year 6 student) _____

Christine (Year 6 student) _____

Scenario: The four Year 6 students are talking at lunch time about how their good friend Olivia is leaving today for another school.

James: This is her last day!

Grant: We should have done something sooner.

Tom: Well, luckily Christine and I did – we made her a card.

Christine: Here's a pen, go sign it and get back here quickly. Next time, plan ahead.

James: Okay, thanks you two. We'll be right back.

Discussion — **Learning from the scenarios**

Choose one student to lead the class through the questions on the Discussion 12 cue card (see below).

Discussion 12 cue card

How did Tom and Christine show great leadership in the second scenario?

How could the students have been more organised, even in the second scenario?

What could each student have done to ensure everyone signed the card on time?

Lesson 11: Planning ahead

≋ Activity **Looking ahead**

Just as it's important for students to plan ahead, they will gain much from reflecting on their leadership journey and all they have learnt throughout the year. Ask each student to:

- create a collage, scrapbook, poster or video of "the year that was" (perhaps as part of their digital learning portfolio)
- interview each other to discover more about their fellow students now and what great plans they have for the future. Video these interviews so that they become treasured memories for years to come.

Possible interview questions

Please tell me about you and your family.	What advice would you like to give to your parents?
Who are some of your friends?	What scares you the most?
What do you like most about your friends?	What makes a great friend?
What sports do you like to play?	If you could meet anyone in the world, who would it be and why?
What are your favourite foods?	What are some of your learning goals for the next year?
What makes you feel the happiest?	
Who is your hero and why?	What would you like to be or do when you grow up?

Daily reminder

Mention the idea of *planning ahead* as much as possible to reinforce this concept whenever there is a teachable moment. If you notice students planning their work, compliment them on their leadership skills and ask them to record any such occasion in their copy of My Leadership Journal on a weekly or daily basis. If you notice an activity or context in which students need to plan ahead more, ask them, "Do you remember the leadership skill called planning ahead? It's when a person takes some time to think about what needs to be done before they do it. I know you, and I believe you can plan ahead. Could you please show me that you are a great leader and that you can plan your work so it gets done properly?"

Involving parents and carers: newsletter blurb

Leadership words of the month: Planning ahead

As you know, we have a whole-school focus on improving student leadership because we believe every child is a leader. This month, our leadership theme is to *plan ahead* as great leaders need to prepare for any important action or event.

If you notice your child planning ahead at home, please congratulate them and consider jotting this incident down in their copy of My Leadership Journal or writing a note for their teacher to post on the class Leadership Ladder poster.

Thanks and we hope you have a great weekend. ☺

My Leadership Journal

How to assemble the journal

Although on first sight the journal may *look* a bit tricky to put together, it's actually quite easy if you follow the steps below in order. If you double-side it, this booklet should use only two pieces of paper.

Here's what you need to do:

1. Photocopy one single-sided copy of the four template sheets for My Leadership Journal (from the following pages).
2. Photocopy your four pages using the double-sided feature (pairing templates A and B; and templates C and D), resulting in two double-sided pages. Once copied, the letters on the top should match up in the order A, B, C and D.
3. Cut each sheet in half horizontally along the dashed line.
4. Fold the sheets vertically down the middle.
5. Assemble the pages in the correct order.
6, Staple the journal together.

Congratulations – you've just made your booklet. ☺

Tips

- You may find it useful to ask for some responsible leaders to assist you with the assembly process.
- As students will need to use this journal throughout the school year, it may help to print a few extra copies for new students, as well as for any students who lose theirs. To limit such losses, emphasise the leadership skill of being responsible, and consider sending the journal home only occasionally.

Template A

My Leadership Journal

My record of times when I showed great leadership

Name: _____

Year: _____

Climbing the Leadership Ladder

Times when I listened

Date   What happened

_____ _____
_____ _____
_____ _____
_____ _____
_____ _____
_____ _____

Peer comments

I saw _____ being a leader.

Date   Comment

_____ _____
_____ _____
_____ _____
_____ _____
_____ _____

© TTS Group Ltd, 2012   53

Template B

Parent comments
Please note down any occasion when you see your child showing great leadership at home.

Date   Comment

_____
_____
_____
_____
_____

15

What I have learnt about being a leader

A great leader is _____
_____

My leadership strengths are _____
_____

Important leadership skills I am going to work on are _____
_____

13

Student Leadership Code

1. I am a great leader.
2. I help others.
3. I do the right thing even when no one is looking.
4. I plan ahead and think of solutions.
5. I encourage others to do the right thing.

2

Times when I showed empathy

Date   What happened

_____
_____
_____
_____
_____
_____

4

---

54   © TTS Group Ltd, 2012

Template C

Times when I had a great attitude	Times when I planned ahead
Date What happened	Date What happened

Times when I had enthusiasm	Times when I used humour well
Date What happened	Date What happened

© TTS Group Ltd, 2012

Template D

Times when I was determined to achieve something positive

Date   What happened

Times when I behaved with integrity

Date   What happened

Times when I behaved responsibly

Date   What happened

Times when I made sensible choices

Date   What happened